DISCARD

D1231975

DRUG ADDICTION AND RECOVERY

Alcohol and Tobacco

Alcohol and Tobacco

H.W. Poole

SERIES CONSULTANT
SARA BECKER, Ph.D.
Brown University School of Public Health
Warren Alpert Medical School

MASON CREST

Mason Crest
450 Parkway Drive, Suite D
Broomall, PA 19008
www.masoncrest.com

MTM Publishing, Inc.
www.mtmpublishing.com

President: Valerie Tomaselli
Vice President, Book Development: Hilary Poole
Designer: Annemarie Redmond
Copyeditor: Peter Jaskowiak
Editorial Assistant: Andrea St. Aubin

Series ISBN: 978-1-4222-3598-0
Hardback ISBN: 978-1-4222-3599-7
E-Book ISBN: 978-1-4222-8243-4

Cataloging-in-Publication Data on file with the Library of Congress

Printed and bound in the United States of America.

First printing
9 8 7 6 5 4 3 2 1

QR CODES AND LINKS TO THIRD PARTY CONTENT
You may gain access to certain third party content ("Third Party Sites") by scanning and using the QR Codes that appear in this publication (the "QR Codes"). We do not operate or control in any respect any information, products or services on such Third Party Sites linked to by us via the QR Codes included in this publication and we assume no responsibility for any materials you may access using the QR Codes. Your use of the QR Codes may be subject to terms, limitations, or restrictions set forth in the applicable terms of use or otherwise established by the owners of the Third Party Sites. Our linking to such Third Party Sites via the QR Codes does not imply an endorsement or sponsorship of such Third Party Sites, or the information, products or services offered on or through the Third Party Sites, nor does it imply an endorsement or sponsorship of this publication by the owners of such Third Party Sites.

TABLE OF CONTENTS

Key Icons to Look for:

Words to Understand: These words with their easy-to-understand definitions will increase the reader's understanding of the text, while building vocabulary skills.

Sidebars: This boxed material within the main text allows readers to build knowledge, gain insights, explore possibilities, and broaden their perspectives by weaving together additional information to provide realistic and holistic perspectives.

Research Projects: Readers are pointed toward areas of further inquiry connected to each chapter. Suggestions are provided for projects that encourage deeper research and analysis.

Text-Dependent Questions: These questions send the reader back to the text for more careful attention to the evidence presented there.

Educational Videos: Readers can view videos by scanning our QR codes, providing them with additional educational content to supplement the text. Examples include news coverage, moments in history, speeches, iconic sports moments and much more!

Series Glossary of Key Terms: This back-of-the-book glossary contains terminology used throughout the series. Words found here increase the reader's ability to read and comprehend higher-level books and articles in this field.

SERIES INTRODUCTION

Many adolescents in the United States will experiment with alcohol or other drugs by time they finish high school. According to a 2014 study funded by the National Institute on Drug Abuse, about 27 percent of 8th graders have tried alcohol, 20 percent have tried drugs, and 13 percent have tried cigarettes. By 12th grade, these rates more than double: 66 percent of 12th graders have tried alcohol, 50 percent have tried drugs, and 35 percent have tried cigarettes.

Adolescents who use substances experience an increased risk of a wide range of negative consequences, including physical injury, family conflict, school truancy, legal problems, and sexually transmitted diseases. Higher rates of substance use are also associated with the leading causes of death in this age group: accidents, suicide, and violent crime. Relative to adults, adolescents who experiment with alcohol or other drugs progress more quickly to a full-blown substance use disorder and have more co-occurring mental health problems.

The National Survey on Drug Use and Health (NSDUH) estimated that in 2015 about 1.3 million adolescents between the ages of 12 and 17 (5 percent of adolescents in the United States) met the medical criteria for a substance use disorder. Unfortunately, the vast majority of these

IF YOU NEED HELP NOW . . .

SAMHSA's National Helpline provides referrals for mental-health or substance-use counseling.
1-800-662-HELP (4357) or https://findtreatment.samhsa.gov

SAMHSA's National Suicide Prevention Lifeline provides crisis counseling by phone or online, 24-hours-a-day and 7 days a week.
1-800-273-TALK (8255) or http://www.suicidepreventionlifeline.org

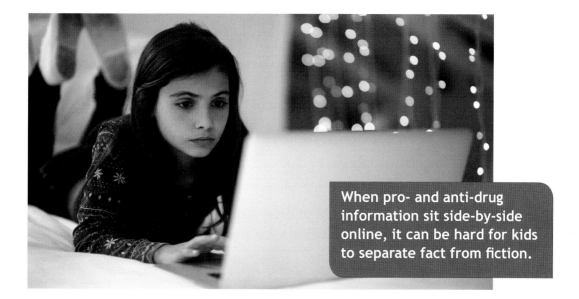

When pro- and anti-drug information sit side-by-side online, it can be hard for kids to separate fact from fiction.

adolescents did not receive treatment. Less than 10 percent of those with a diagnosis received specialty care, leaving 1.2 million adolescents with an unmet need for treatment.

The NSDUH asked the 1.2 million adolescents with untreated substance use disorders why they didn't receive specialty care. Over 95 percent said that they didn't think they needed it. The other 5 percent reported challenges finding quality treatment that was covered by their insurance. Very few treatment providers and agencies offer substance use treatment designed to meet the specific needs of adolescents. Meanwhile, numerous insurance plans have "opted out" of providing coverage for addiction treatment, while others have placed restrictions on what is covered.

Stigma about substance use is another serious problem. We don't call a person with an eating disorder a "food abuser," but we use terms like "drug abuser" to describe individuals with substance use disorders. Even treatment providers often unintentionally use judgmental words, such as describing urine screen results as either "clean" or "dirty." Underlying this language is the idea that a substance use disorder is some kind of moral failing or character flaw, and that people with these disorders deserve blame or punishment for their struggles.

And punish we do. A 2010 report by CASA Columbia found that in the United States, 65 percent of the 2.3 million people in prisons and jails met medical criteria for a substance use disorder, while another 20 percent had histories of substance use disorders, committed their crimes while under the influence of alcohol or drugs, or committed a substance-related crime. Many of these inmates spend decades in prison, but only 11 percent of them receive any treatment during their incarceration. Our society invests significantly more money in punishing individuals with substance use disorders than we do in treating them.

At a basic level, the ways our society approaches drugs and alcohol—declaring a "war on drugs," for example, or telling kids to "Just Say No!"—reflect a misunderstanding about the nature of addiction. The reality is that addiction is a disease that affects all types of people—parents and children, rich and poor, young and old. Substance use disorders stem from a complex interplay of genes, biology, and the environment, much like most physical and mental illnesses.

The way we talk about recovery, using phrases like "kick the habit" or "breaking free," also misses the mark. Substance use disorders are chronic, insidious, and debilitating illnesses. Fortunately, there are a number of effective treatments for substance use disorders. For many patients, however, the road is long and hard. Individuals recovering from substance use disorders can experience horrible withdrawal symptoms, and many will continue to struggle with cravings for alcohol or drugs. It can be a daily struggle to cope with these cravings and stay abstinent. A popular saying at Alcoholics Anonymous (AA) meetings is "one day at a time," because every day of recovery should be respected and celebrated.

There are a lot of incorrect stereotypes about individuals with substance use disorders, and there is a lot of false information about the substances, too. If you do an Internet search on the term "marijuana," for instance, two top hits are a web page by the National Institute on Drug Abuse and a page operated by Weedmaps, a medical and recreational marijuana dispensary. One of these pages publishes scientific information and one publishes pro-marijuana articles. Both pages have a high-quality, professional appearance. If you had never heard of either organization, it would be hard to know which to trust. It can be really difficult for the average person, much less the average teenager, to navigate these waters.

The topics covered in this series were specifically selected to be relevant to teenagers. About half of the volumes cover the types of drugs that they are most likely to hear about or to come in contact with. The other half cover important issues related to alcohol and other drug use (which we refer to as "drug use" in the titles for simplicity). These books cover topics such as the causes of drug use, the influence of drug use on the family, drug use and the legal system, drug use and mental health, and treatment options. Many teens will either have personal experience with these issues or will know someone who does.

This series was written to help young people get the facts about common drugs, substance use disorders, substance-related problems, and recovery. Accurate information can help adolescents to make better decisions. Students who are educated can help each other to better understand the risks and consequences of drug use. Facts also go a long way to reducing the stigma associated with substance use. We tend to fear or avoid things that we don't understand. Knowing the facts can make it easier to support each other. For students who know someone struggling with a substance use disorder, these books can also help them know what to expect. If they are worried about someone, or even about themselves, these books can help to provide some answers and a place to start.

—Sara J. Becker, Ph.D., Assistant Professor (Research), Center for Alcohol and Addictions Studies, Brown University School of Public Health, Assistant Professor (Research), Department of Psychiatry and Human Behavior, Brown University Medical School

WORDS TO UNDERSTAND

abstention: actively choosing to not do something.

ambivalence: mixed feelings, both good and bad.

bootlegger: someone who makes alcohol illegally.

distilled: purified.

Prohibition: the years 1920 to 1933, when it was illegal to sell alcohol in the United States.

temperance: self-restraint; here, it refers specifically to a historical movement focused on avoiding alcohol.

CHAPTER ONE

ALCOHOL AND SOCIETY

Alcohol and tobacco are often discussed together—as they are in this book—because they are legal drugs that are both frequently used in social settings. But there's a huge difference between them: while you might hear about "safe" amounts of alcohol, there is no "safe" amount of tobacco. It's well known that smoking is unhealthy, and that the best thing any smoker can do is quit. The question of whether smoking is good or bad is easily answered: it's not just bad, it's *very* bad. (See chapters four and five for more on tobacco, nicotine, and smoking.)

The situation with alcohol is much different. Many factors come into play, some biological (like age, gender, and family history) and some social (like religion and community standards). Ambivalence about alcohol is nothing new. The truth is, human beings and alcohol have a long, complicated relationship. And the line between "acceptable" and "unacceptable" alcohol consumption has continued to evolve and change

Young people get a lot of mixed messages when it comes to alcohol. On the one hand, adults lecture them to stay away from it, while on the other hand, many adults themselves seem to make alcohol a key part of their social lives.

over time. The social history of drinking is the story of a constant push-pull between indulgence and abstention.

ANCIENT ALCOHOL

The first type of alcoholic drink made by humans was probably beer. For example, the workers and slaves who built the pyramids of Giza were given beer as part of their daily rations. Beer was also was made by Sumerians around 3200 BCE. (Sumer was in southern Mesopotamia, in modern Iraq.) Sumerians made wine about 200 years later, but evidence suggests that beer remained the more popular drink. In fact, the first recipe recorded in human history was for a type of beer.

Wine was much more popular in ancient Greece, where it was a key part of people's social lives. Ancient cultures on the Indian subcontinent also made alcohol around 500 BCE, although archaeologists believe this was probably used as part of medical practice, rather than socially.

Romans seem to have used alcohol for both purposes—medicinal and recreational. For example, the Roman doctor Galen, around 170 CE, used wine to disinfect wounds while he worked as a physician to gladiators. When it came to wine for drinking, the beverages Romans consumed were almost always diluted with water or some other ingredient. Romans almost never consumed pure wine, as people do today. In fact, the very idea was considered uncivilized.

Amphorae were special casks made by Ancient Greeks for transporting liquids such as wine and olive oil. These are on display in a Turkish museum after being rescued from a shipwreck.

HAMMURABI

The Code of Hammurabi, which dates back to about 1754 BCE, is the first-known set of laws. King Hammurabi is probably most famous for giving us the concept of "an eye for an eye." Less famously, among its hundreds of different laws, the Code has rules related to alcohol. For example, it has a provision about prices for wine, and about paying for wine with money versus paying with grain. The Code also states that if a "sister of god," (a nun, in modern language) either opens or even enters a tavern, she can be put to death by fire.

ALCOHOL AND PROHIBITION

While many (although not all) cultures have embraced alcohol for medical, religious, and social uses, there has also been a longstanding awareness of the risks. This tension can be seen, for example, in the teachings of the Catholic Church around the 17th century: on the one hand, alcohol was considered a gift from God and was to be enjoyed; on the other hand, "drunkenness" was viewed as sinful.

Around this time, distilled liquors became increasingly popular. For example, the colonial American economy became increasingly dependent on rum sales (another key product was tobacco; see chapter four). Back in England, laws were passed to encourage domestic gin production. In 1730, about 10 million gallons of gin were made in London alone. This "gin craze," as it came to be called, was blamed for increasing social problems, including crime, child neglect, and prostitution. A nobleman named Lord John Hervey observed that "the whole town of London swarmed with drunken people from morning to night." And so, the same British government that had deliberately encouraged gin production now found itself condemning it. The Gin Act of 1736 placed high taxes on the liquor, but this mainly led to legitimate gin makers going out of business, while bootleggers thrived.

A similar situation occurred later in the United States. In the 1800s, a boom in immigration brought large numbers of new Americans from Western European countries, where drinking was extremely common. Beer gardens, for example, were a huge part of daily life in Germany. Immigrants brought their traditions with them to the United States. Meanwhile, the country was swept with a religious revival movement that considered drinking alcohol to be a sin. A powerful temperance movement emerged in response.

After many decades of organizing and protesting, activists succeeded in pushing through the Eighteenth Amendment to the U.S. Constitution, which made it illegal to make or sell alcoholic beverages. In theory, Prohibition would not only reduce drinking, but it would also reduce the social problems that come with it, such as crime. But this "noble experiment,"

The "Ohio Whiskey War" took place in the 1870s; temperance advocates sang hymns outside drinking establishments.

In New York City around 1921, illegal liquor is poured into the sewers as officials look on.

as it was sometimes called, failed on both counts. Prohibition did not stop the flow of alcohol, and it certainly did not reduce crime. In fact, it mainly succeeded in creating criminal bootlegging operations like the one run by Chicago's Al Capone. Prohibition was repealed in 1933, led by the newly elected president, Franklin Roosevelt, who had made repeal a key part of his political platform.

ALCOHOL IN MODERN SOCIETY

It may seem like alcohol is impossible to escape these days. And yet the messages we receive about drinking are contradictory. We are bombarded by media images that promote alcohol as part of a hip or carefree lifestyle, but we also constantly hear about the health and

TEMPERANCE AND WOMEN'S RIGHTS

The American temperance movement is noteworthy for the fact that it was organized and run largely by women. Connecting temperance and women's rights might seem odd now, but in the 19th and 20th centuries, it made complete sense. At the time, women had almost no legal or political power. If a woman's husband spent all the family money on drinking, or if he got drunk and abused his wife or children, there was very little that the average woman could do about it. So while the temperance movement failed to stop alcohol consumption, it was important in at least one way: many women got interested in politics because of temperance. Soon they would turn their attention—and newfound organizing skills—to winning women the right to vote.

safety risks involved. This can be tough for young people to navigate. On the one hand, they get lectured about abstaining; on the other hand, when they look around, it doesn't look like other people are doing much abstaining at all.

This situation is more complex than you might think. According to the 2014 National Survey on Drug Use and Health (NSDUH), 81.5 percent of Americans over the age of 12 are estimated to have consumed alcohol at some point in their lives. But only 66.6 percent reported they had consumed any in the previous year, and only 52.7 had consumed any in the month before the survey was taken. That's a lot of Americans, to be sure—but it's hardly "everybody," as the media might have you believe.

Not every culture is a drinking culture. For example, some religions strongly disapprove of alcohol consumption. The Mormon faith forbids the drinking of alcohol because of "the law of health," which has been a part of Mormonism since 1833. In the Islamic faith, alcohol is likewise *haram*, or "forbidden."

A bronze statue of Joseph Smith, the founder of Mormonism. The Mormon prohibition on alcohol comes from Smith's "law of health" from 1833.

There are also more than 500 "dry counties" in the United States. "Dry," in this context, means that the sale of alcoholic beverages is prohibited in these areas. Towns and counties can choose to "go dry," usually by passing a public referendum on the subject. Some of these communities forbade alcohol long before Prohibition, while others simply opted to leave Prohibition in place after it was repealed.

However, the overall trend seems to be toward ending these laws. This is in great part a question of economics. Towns and counties sometimes find they need the income that would come from alcohol taxes, as well as increased business to their restaurants and hotels. In 2013, for example, voters in Seneca, New York, threw out a ban on alcohol sales that had been on the books since the early 19th century.

TEXT-DEPENDENT QUESTIONS

1. What were the earliest alcoholic beverages, and who made them?
2. What was the Gin Act? Why was it passed and what were the results?
3. What are some communities or cultures that abstain from alcohol?

RESEARCH PROJECT

Find out more about the history of the Eighteenth Amendment to the U.S. Constitution. Write a short editorial from the perspective of a temperance activist, listing the various reasons why the amendment was a good idea. Then write a second editorial from the perspective of an anti-temperance campaigner, listing the various reasons why the amendment should be repealed. Which argument do you find more persuasive?

WORDS TO UNDERSTAND

chronic: ongoing or recurring.

cognitive: having to do with thought.

craving: a very strong desire for something.

depressant: a substance that slows particular bodily functions.

inhibit: to limit or hold back.

predisposition: to be more inclined or likely to do something.

prognosis: the probable outcome of a disease.

CHAPTER TWO

ALCOHOL—EFFECTS AND TREATMENT

C_2H_5OH: two molecules of carbon, five of hydrogen, one of oxygen, and another of hydrogen. Together, they make a compound called ethyl alcohol, which is the most important ingredient in any alcoholic beverage.

There are many other types of alcohol. For example, there's the liquid that you might find in a first-aid kit. But that type of alcohol would be toxic to drink. During Prohibition, bootleggers made "moonshine" in bathtubs, and some of those folks went blind or even died because the type of alcohol they made, called methanol, was poisonous. So while there are many types of alcohol, there's only one—C_2H_5OH—that is consumable by humans.

You'd never know this by looking at alcohol advertisements. Companies that make and sell alcoholic drinks spend vast amounts of money on creating the impression that their products are totally different from the competition. But from the first alcohol created thousands of years ago to the high-end wineries of today, every alcoholic beverage is, on a basic level, the same.

THE EFFECTS OF ALCOHOL

When a person takes a drink, the alcohol goes into the stomach and is absorbed into the bloodstream. Although we think about how alcohol affects our brains, it actually affects the entire body. This is especially important for women who are pregnant, because if a pregnant woman is drinking, her baby is drinking, too. Also, people who drink heavily for many years will begin to have problems with their livers and digestive systems. Even some forms of cancer are associated with alcohol exposure. That said, it's true that alcohol is best absorbed by the fatty tissues of the brain. That's why alcohol has such a big impact on how people feel and behave.

One aspect of alcohol that can be confusing is the fact that it's a depressant. That might be surprising, since people tend to drink alcohol in social situations like parties. But "depressant" doesn't necessarily mean "depressed." Alcohol slows down bodily functions, and that includes how well the brain works. At low doses, this can make people feel more

This woodcut from a German medical text suggests that the effects of alcohol were well-known to people even in the 16th century.

relaxed and outgoing, because their anxieties are reduced. But these good feelings come at a cost: brains that are influenced by alcohol are less able to form memories or to think in complex ways. It's pretty common for people to make bad decisions— about sex, for example, or other risky behavior—while under the influence of alcohol.

In addition to decision making, reaction times are also harmed by alcohol. There is a bigger gap between the moment when a person sees or hears something and the moment when the person reacts. This is why it's so dangerous for someone who has been drinking to drive a car.

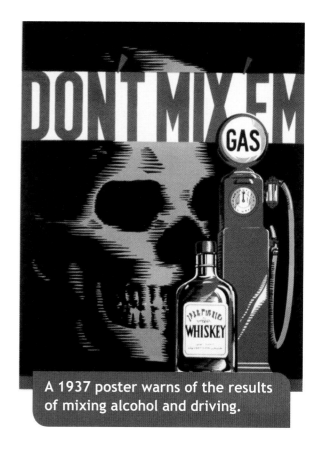

A 1937 poster warns of the results of mixing alcohol and driving.

It's all too common for people to have several drinks and think, "I'm fine, I don't feel drunk at all." But even if they don't "feel drunk," they may react too slowly to conditions on the road—things like traffic lights or a sudden stop by the car in front of them. According to the Centers for Disease Control and Prevention (CDC), almost 30 people die in alcohol-related accidents every single day. That works out to one death every 51 minutes.

At higher doses, alcohol **inhibits** muscle coordination. That's where the expression "falling down drunk" comes from; people really do lose the ability to make their arms and legs work the way they want. The brain also stops receiving signals from the body that relate to touch and pain. That's why drunk people can easily hurt themselves and not even realize it until much later. And at even higher doses, basic functions like breathing and heart rate also slow down—in extreme cases, to the point of coma or death.

ALCOHOL MISUSE

Many adults drink alcohol on special occasions like holidays, or maybe casually with friends after work. Much of that type of alcohol consumption is sometimes called "social drinking." This term refers to the practice of enjoying alcohol in social situations. But the term can be a bit of a trap, especially for young people. It seems to imply that social drinking is the "good" kind of drinking, while the opposite—drinking "antisocially" or alone —is the "bad" kind of drinking. You might have even heard people say something along these lines, like, "I only drink at parties," or "I don't have a problem because I don't drink alone." But the truth is, how many people happen to be in the room has nothing to do alcoholism. It is completely possible for someone with a drinking problem to "only" drink socially.

Because alcohol has such a strong effect on the brain, it's very easy for people to end up having more drinks than they intended. Also, some people grow to rely on alcohol all the time; in fact, they feel unhappy or downright ill if they *don't* have any (see sidebar on page 25). Some people have a genetic **predisposition** toward alcohol misuse. Others drink as a way of "self-medicating"—helping ease anxiety, for example, or in an attempt to cheer themselves up. If a person starts to feel that alcohol is no longer "optional" but is actually "required," that may signal the beginnings of a problem.

ALCOHOL USE DISORDER

You've probably heard someone say that so-and-so "has a drinking problem" or "is an alcoholic." These terms get thrown around a lot in the media, to the point where you might wonder what they even mean in practical terms.

WITHDRAWAL SYMPTOMS

Alcohol is a socially acceptable drug, but it's still a drug. And like any drug, the human body can become dependent on it. When that occurs—when the body becomes accustomed to having regular "doses" of alcohol—there will be physical repercussions if person tries to stop "cold turkey." These are called withdrawal symptoms, and they can range from mild to severe, depending on how dependent an individual is. The expected withdrawal symptoms, according to the U.S. National Library of Medicine, are as follows:

- anxiety
- depression
- fatigue
- irritability
- jumpiness or shakiness
- mood swings
- nightmares
- not thinking clearly
- clammy skin

- enlarged (dilated) pupils
- insomnia
- loss of appetite
- nausea and vomiting
- pallor
- rapid heart rate
- sweating
- tremor of the hands or other body parts

The most severe type of alcohol withdrawal is called delirium tremens (DTs). Its symptoms include agitation and confusion, fever, hallucinations, and seizures.

The medical profession has a set of criteria that it uses to diagnose drinking problems. The symptoms are explained in the *Diagnostic and Statistical Manual of Mental Disorders*, now in its 5th edition (*DSM-5*).

The formal name for "drinking problem" is alcohol use disorder. The symptoms include things like drinking more than originally intended, trying and failing to stop drinking, **craving** alcohol and being upset if none is available, and having problems at home or school that are tied to drinking

People often assume that heavy drinkers have to "hit bottom" before starting treatment, but this is a myth.

and/or hangovers. The more symptoms a person has, the more serious the disorder is said to be. The NSDUH reports that in 2013, 2.8 percent of young people (aged 12 to 17) and 7.0 percent of adults in the United States suffered from an alcohol use disorder.

The media has created an impression that if someone gets treatment for an alcohol use disorder, it must mean that his or her life is a complete disaster. But this is not accurate at all. Alcohol use disorders are very treatable, and there is no need to wait. Particularly when it comes to teenagers, the sooner someone gets help, the better their prognosis will be.

TREATMENT OPTIONS

There are several types of treatment for alcohol use disorders: some involve medical professionals, and some don't. Because other disorders—such as anxiety or depression—often occur hand-in-hand with alcohol misuse, one of the first things doctors often do is assess whether there are co-occurring psychological disorders. Depending on the situation, a medical professional might decide to address the other disorder first. For example, if someone is drinking to reduce feelings of anxiety around peers, then treating the person's underlying social anxiety might make it easier for that person to then cut back on his or her drinking.

As far as alcohol use disorders go, the best-studied type of treatment is called cognitive-behavioral therapy (CBT). The term *cognitive* refers to the human thought process—how people think. And, of course, *behavioral* refers to how people act. So CBT involves adjusting both how people think about their substance use and the choices they make to act (or not act) on those thoughts.

For example, CBT encourages people to better understand the choices they make. What is it they like about drinking, and what are they getting out of it? How can these needs be addressed in more productive, less harmful ways? People in CBT learn about their personal triggers—settings, people, or events that make them want to drink. They then learn to avoid or cope with those triggers. That probably sounds simple, but it can actually be very challenging. For example, imagine if stress at school is a trigger. Teens can't simply skip school just to avoid their triggers. So CBT teaches new ways to function in that environment to cope with the triggers and make healthier decisions.

CBT is a lot of work—in fact, there's often homework involved! It also takes time. But it has been shown to be effective in helping people take more control of their choices and lives. Some experts recommend CBT be done in conjunction with a medicine called naltrexone, which helps ease physical cravings for alcohol.

Another short-term type of treatment is called motivational enhancement therapy (MET). MET sometimes involves "interviews" between the therapist and the patient. Rather than being judgmental or confrontational, the therapist treats the patient with empathy, exploring the reasons behind his or her alcohol use. Importantly, the therapist tries to help the patient understand how drinking might get in the way of the patient's long-term goals, like going to college, winning an athletic scholarship, or even finding a boyfriend or girlfriend. Chronic alcohol use will to make such goals harder—sometimes impossible—to achieve.

SUPPORT GROUPS

For many people who have recovered from alcohol-use disorders, support groups were a key element of their success. Alcoholics Anonymous (AA) is the most famous, but there are other programs, too. Some, such as Smart Recovery, mix peer support with CBT techniques. Although recovery programs vary, they all tend to be based around the same basic ideas: peer support, managing cravings and triggers, and maintaining a healthy life without alcohol.

The roots of AA go back to a religious organization known as the Oxford Group. Members of the Oxford Group spoke of surrendering their lives to God, and of living by the "four absolutes" of honesty, purity, unselfishness, and love. Their self-improvement practices included prayer and meditation, admitting wrongs and making amends, and bringing their ideas to others. All these ideas became the bedrock of AA, which was founded in 1935 by Oxford Group members Bill Wilson and Robert Smith. Because anonymity is such an important component of AA meetings, the founders are more famously known as Bill W and Dr. Bob. The AA program is based on a series of "12 steps" toward recovery. AA members have to admit to their drinking, for example, and then make it up to people who've been hurt by their behavior.

Peer support can be a very helpful and important part of therapy.

For all its success, AA does have its critics. Some people find the religious component of the group off-putting. As a result, a number of "secular AA" groups have been formed to offer programs that are similar to AA's but without the religious component.

One key idea of AA is that "some forces are beyond our control," and some critics argue that a sense of helplessness can be counterproductive when it comes to battling addiction. The very first of the 12 steps says that "our lives [have] become unmanageable," but many doctors would prefer that their patients got into treatment well before the point of "unmanageable" is reached. Further, the AA slogan that "the program works if you work it" is sometimes criticized for creating an unrealistic expectation of success. It can sometimes make people feel like hopeless failures if, in fact, the program *doesn't* work for them. Although exact numbers are not available, research suggests that AA works well for people who seek the program out, but less well for people who are forced to attend meetings (by a judge, for example).

TEXT-DEPENDENT QUESTIONS

1. What parts of the body does alcohol affect?
2. What is cognitive-behavioral therapy?
3. What are some of the foundational ideas of 12-step programs?

RESEARCH PROJECT

Write up a guide to getting help for alcohol dependence that gives specific information about your community. Find out what programs are available in your school, church, or neighborhood.

WORDS TO UNDERSTAND

binge: doing something to excess.

deterioration: becoming worse.

hippocampus: a part of the brain involved in emotions and memories.

limbic system: a complex brain system that controls a person's instincts, basic emotions, and moods.

CHAPTER THREE

ALCOHOL AND TEENS

We often contrast drugs like alcohol and cigarettes with drugs like cocaine and heroin, noting that the former are "legal" and the latter are "illegal." But that's not completely true. Alcohol and cigarettes actually *are* illegal drugs if used by young people. In the United States, alcohol is restricted to use by people over the age of 21, and cigarettes are restricted to 18 or 19 depending on the state. In Canada and Mexico, both alcohol and cigarettes are restricted to 18—or, in a couple of Canadian provinces, 19.

Alcohol consumption by people who are younger than the legal age, otherwise known as "underage drinking," is illegal and, unfortunately, fairly common. In 2014 the NSDUH found that almost 30 percent of kids between 12 and 17 had tried alcohol at some point in their lives, 24 percent had consumed it in the previous year, and 11.5 percent had consumed it in the previous month. According to the National Institutes of Health, more than 4,300 people under age 21 die every year from factors related to alcohol use—that includes alcohol-related car accidents as well as suicides,

Especially for college kids, alcohol might sometimes feel like an unavoidable part of socializing.

poisoning, drowning, falls, and other causes. The number of hospital visits for underage drinkers is estimated to approach 200,000 every year.

Despite these statistics, it's pretty common for teens to wonder why having an occasional beer is "such a big deal." But the laws make more sense if you understand some key differences between adults and teens.

GROWING BRAINS

Teens tend to stop growing taller at around 15 or 16 years old. There are exceptions to this, but in general, how tall you are at 16 is *roughly* how tall you're going to be. However, just because that aspect of your growth is mostly over, that doesn't mean you aren't growing in other, less visible ways. The human brain continues to develop until people are well into their 20s.

Alcohol can do more damage to the brain of a teenager than to an adult because the teenager's brain is still developing. In a paper published by the National Institute on Alcohol Abuse and Alcoholism (NIAAA), researchers described the adolescent brain as "uniquely sensitive" to alcohol exposure. The paper concluded, "Alcohol exposure during adolescence can have long-lasting effects and may interfere with normal brain functioning during adulthood."

Alcohol has an effect on many different parts of the brain. The cerebral cortex, where information from the five senses is processed, is slowed down by alcohol. The frontal lobes, which guide decision making, planning, and self-control, are also inhibited. The hippocampus, which is a small but vital part of the limbic system is especially affected by drinking.

One of the big jobs of the hippocampus is to form memories. When the hippocampus is damaged, it gets harder or even impossible for memories to be formed. For instance, one of the early symptoms of Alzheimer's disease is memory trouble. That's because the disease harms the hippocampus first. Alcohol can damage the hippocampus. In one study, researchers looked at brain scans of heavy drinkers and found a noticeable reduction in the size of the hippocampus compared to nondrinkers.

Teen brains are especially sensitive to alcohol when it comes to memory. In another study from 1998, people between the ages of 20 and 29 consumed alcohol and were then given lists of words to memorize. In general, the participants were able to repeat the words initially, but many were unable to remember them 20 minutes later. Here's the most important part: the study found that the younger the people were, the *more likely* they were to have trouble retaining the information. In other words, the effects of alcohol on memory were observed to be stronger in younger people.

TEEN PSYCHOLOGY

In addition to questions of physical development, there are psychological reasons why drinking by young people is of great concern. First, adolescence is a time of experimentation and risk-taking. Kids who drink often take much bigger risks than they should, getting themselves into situations they are not prepared to handle. For example, kids who've been drinking can end up starting fights, trying harder drugs that they would have avoided if they were sober, or having sex before they are ready. In addition, the mistakes people make under the influence of alcohol can be permanent. One of the worst things a drinking teen can do is simply get behind the wheel of a car. A teen driver who has been drinking is *17 times more likely* to die in a crash than a teen driving sober.

Second, the practice of **binge** drinking is all too common. Binge drinking is defined as consuming many drinks in one sitting (four drinks for females, or five for males). This is a common social activity, especially among college students. As one student told an interviewer for National Public Radio, "There's no 'I'm going to have a buzz and I'll be OK,' . . . they drink as much as they can take in before either blacking out or passing out." And if that's what your friends like to do at a party, there can be a lot of pressure to join in.

Finally, underage drinking sets kids up to become problem drinkers later. The younger kids are when they start drinking, the more likely they are to develop chronic alcohol use disorders later in life.

SPECIAL ISSUES FOR TEENS IN RECOVERY

The discussion about recovery in the previous chapter also applies to teenagers, but there are a few special issues involved that are worth considering. One big difference between teens and adults with alcohol use disorders is that young people are frequently still living at home. This might make the situation more challenging, since family problems can contribute to alcohol misuse.

At the same time, the fact that teens are usually still at home can be a huge opportunity. If parents are willing to participate in therapy, the additional support for their kids may make a huge difference in helping teens stick with their treatments. The NIAAA says that there is a large "unmet need" for

HANGOVERS AND TEENS

It's clear that alcohol can affect developing brains in profound and long-term ways. But there is something else interesting going on when it comes to alcohol and young people. It turns out that although teens are more susceptible to brain damage due to alcohol consumption, they are actually less affected by certain other aspects of alcohol use.

Laboratory experiments have suggested that the younger animals are, the less likely they are to experience deterioration in muscle coordination while under the influence of alcohol. (Usually, rats and mice are used in these experiments, because it is unethical to experiment on actual teenagers.) Younger animals are also less likely to pass out from the effects of alcohol, compared to older animals. Hangovers, which can be pretty terrible for adults, also don't seem to impact teens quite so strongly.

Sounds great, right? Not exactly. Hangovers serve as a useful motivation for people to limit their consumption, simply because they don't want to be miserable the next morning. Because teens don't experience that as much, and because they are less likely to either fall down or pass out, their bodies don't warn them of the damage they are doing to themselves. The result is that young people have a higher risk of long-term, irreversible problems, even though they have fewer short-term consequences that might inspire them to cut back.

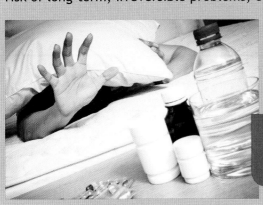

For many, the misery of hangovers is an inducement to drink less.

TEEN QUESTIONS

People who are dependent on alcohol (or other drugs) are frequently in denial. That is, they don't want to admit to others that they have a problem.

The National Council on Alcoholism and Drug Dependence (NCADD) put together a list of questions specifically for teenagers. Answering these questions will help young people assess whether they need help to reduce their drinking.

- Do you use alcohol or other drugs to feel more self-confident, more sociable, or more powerful?
- Do you ever drink or get high immediately after you have a problem at home or at school?
- Have you lost friends because of your alcohol or drug use, or started hanging out with a heavy drinking or drug-using crowd?
- Do you feel guilty or bummed out after using alcohol or other drugs, or ever wake up and wonder what happened the night before?
- Have you gotten into trouble at home or school, missed school, or been busted or hospitalized because of alcohol or other drugs?
- Do your friends use "less" alcohol and/or other drugs than you, or do you consume alcohol or other drugs until your supply is all gone?
- Do you think you have a problem with alcohol or other drugs?

Giving positive answers to a few of these questions does not automatically mean you have an alcohol use disorder—only a doctor can determine that diagnosis. But, if you do answer "yes," consider it an early-warning sign. Consider talking to an adult you trust about your drinking and exploring ways to cut down or stop drinking.

Source: NCADD, "Self-Test for Teenagers." https://www.ncadd.org/get-help/take-the-test/self-test-for-teenagers.

treatment of teens with alcohol problems. Only a small percentage of young people who need help actually get it. Researchers have observed that many traditional treatment programs are not well designed for the specific needs of young people. For example, many teens are not in a position to live at a rehab center for weeks at a time. Instead, they need local programs that allow them to live at home and continue their educations as much as possible.

Programs also need to address the fact that many teens with alcohol use disorders also have other problems. That could mean additional substance use disorders or mental illnesses. The NIAAA recommends that more programs focus on "Screening, Brief Intervention, and Referral to Treatment," or "SBIRT," in settings like schools or emergency rooms. Screening helps detect those teens who most need treatment, while brief interventions can be specifically tailored to the concrete problems a teen might be facing in that moment. Referral to treatment is then designed to ensure that those teens with more serious alcohol problems are linked to ongoing treatment.

TEXT-DEPENDENT QUESTIONS

1. What are some signs of a possible problem with alcohol in teens?
2. What are some of the risks of underage drinking?
3. How many young people die of alcohol-related causes every year?

RESEARCH PROJECT

Find out more about Screening, Brief Intervention, and Referral to Treatment (SBIRT) programs. You might begin your research at the website of the Substance Abuse and Mental Health Services Administration (http://www.samhsa.gov/sbirt). What is the philosophy behind SBIRT? How does it work?

WORDS TO UNDERSTAND

antitrust: legislation that tries to create economic competition between companies.

carcinogenic: something that causes cancer.

regulate: to oversee or control something.

remedial: here, to "remedy" or cure something.

CHAPTER FOUR

TOBACCO AND SOCIETY

Tobacco is one of humankind's oldest drugs. Historians believe the plant was first grown in the Andes Mountains between 5,000 and 3,000 BCE. From there, the plant spread across Latin America. Archaeologists have found carvings of the Mayans using tobacco that date back to somewhere between 600 and 900 CE. Tobacco, which was usually smoked in a pipe, was part of religious ceremonies in many cultures. Many people also chewed the leaves of the plant itself.

When Christopher Columbus reached Bahia Bariay, on the island of Cuba, in 1492, he saw Taino natives smoking what turned out to be tobacco. Columbus brought samples of tobacco back to Europe. At first, the plant was viewed mostly as a curiosity from the "New World." But it did not take long for Europeans to develop an interest in smoking.

Ironically, it was 16th-century physicians who first encouraged the rise of tobacco use across Europe. For example, the Spanish doctor Nicolas Monardes claimed that tobacco could cure almost two-dozen illnesses,

This illustration of native South Americans shows the use of tobacco in a formal ceremony.

including snakebites, toothaches, and—amazingly—cancer. The French ambassador Jean Nicot gave tobacco leaves to Catherine de Medici, who was queen of France at the time, to help ease her migraines. Over two centuries later, in 1828, when scientists discovered the active ingredient in tobacco, they named it *nicotine* after the ambassador.

By and large, tobacco had to be imported from the West Indies. There were some attempts to grow tobacco commercially in Europe, but they failed. But in the warmer climate of the Jamestown colony in the United States, the plant thrived. In 1618, 20,000 pounds of tobacco were grown in Virginia, and by 1640 that amount had soared to 1.5 million pounds. More than any other cash crop, tobacco sales fed and sustained the American colonies for several generations.

> *"Smoking is a custom loathsome to the eye, hateful to the nose, harmful to the brain, [and] dangerous to the lungs."*
>
> —King James I, "A Counterblaste to Tobacco," 1604

THE CIGARETTE REVOLUTION

Until the mid-19th century, tobacco was chewed or smoked in pipes, cigars, and hand-rolled cigarettes. Cigarette rolling was a highly sought-after skill—a good roller could turn out several cigarettes per minute. But as so often happens, technical innovations sparked a revolution. In 1880, James Albert Bonsack invented the first cigarette rolling machine, which could create well over 100,000 cigarettes in a single day.

Bonsack went into business with the Duke family of North Carolina. Washington Duke had founded the first cigarette company in Raleigh, in 1865. In 1878 they founded W. Duke Sons & Co. Their first brand of machine-rolled cigarettes was called Duke of Durham, and it was packaged with baseball cards in order to appeal to young men and boys. They sold 10 million cigarettes in their first year; five years into their business, they'd sold 1 billion.

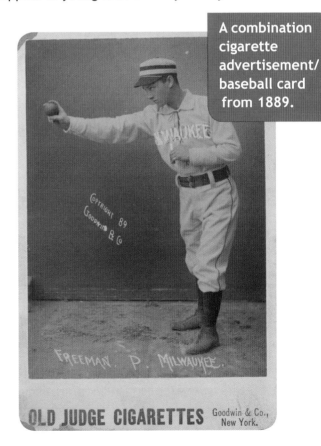

A combination cigarette advertisement/ baseball card from 1889.

OLD JUDGE CIGARETTES   Goodwin & Co., New York.

The company was renamed the American Tobacco Company (ATC) in 1890. The name was appropriate. The company had been busy buying up smaller firms, and before long ATC essentially controlled the cigarette industry in the United States. The company was found guilty of violating antitrust laws in 1911, and U.S. courts forced the company to be broken up into four different companies: ATC, Liggett & Myers, Lorillard, and R.J. Reynolds. R.J. Reynolds, with its famous Camel cigarettes, has remained a major player in the tobacco business.

MARKETING AND ADVERTISING

With ATC split into different companies, the industry thrived. World Wars I and II provided opportunities to hand out cigarettes to soldiers overseas *and* advertise to their wives back at home. And advertise they did. Tobacco companies made some wild claims in the first half of the 20th century. A 1929 print ad for the brand Lucky Strike claimed that "20,679 physicians" had endorsed the product for "throat protection . . . against Cough," while a 1937 Camel ad encouraged people to smoke "for your digestion's sake." Other ads targeted women, claiming that a particular brand would help them "keep a slender figure." But in the second half of the century, things began to change.

Concerns about the health effects of smoking had been building for years. In 1957 the U.S. Surgeon General announced that it was now official U.S. policy to recognize that cigarettes were **carcinogenic**. But the date that would live in infamy—as far as the tobacco industry was concerned—was January 11, 1964. The top news story that day was the publication of the government report called *Smoking and Health,* which described the results of a two-year study of tobacco. The report noted that smokers were up to 10 times more likely to develop lung cancer than nonsmokers. It also highlighted the relationship of smoking to bronchitis, emphysema, and heart disease. The report concluded by saying, "Cigarette smoking is a health hazard of sufficient importance in the United States to warrant appropriate **remedial** action." These actions included a health warning, which was placed on cigarettes in 1965, and a ban on television and radio adverting in 1969.

Publicly, the tobacco industry denied all the claims made against their product. In response to the 1964 report, a representative of Philip Morris, one of the leading U.S. companies, stated, "We don't accept the idea that there are harmful agents in tobacco."

We now know that, in secret, scientists working for the industry had come to the same conclusions even *before* the government scientists. In 1953, for example, an R.J. Reynolds executive wrote that "studies of clinical data tend to confirm the relationship between heavy and prolonged tobacco smoking and incidence of cancer in the lung." In public, however, the industry stood firm in its denial that smoking caused cancer. They also denied that tobacco was addictive and that their ads were targeting young people. The World Health Organization refers to the tobacco companies' cover-up as the "most astonishing systematic corporate deceit of all time."

It is now accepted that tobacco products are dangerous. Public health campaigns have proven effective at reducing the number of Americans who smoke. For example, in 1965, 42 percent of Americans were regular smokers; by 2013, that number was down to 17 percent. Globally, however, the overall number of smokers is increasing. Currently, the global death toll from smoking has been estimated at 4 million people per year. The World Health Organization estimates that 10 million people will die annually by 2030, with 70 percent of those deaths happening in developing countries.

A British advertisement from 1939 shows endorsements from a doctor, a figure skater, and two trapeze artists.

SMOKING AND PUBLIC HEALTH

Governments have tried various methods to induce people to quit smoking. The goal, in the words of the Department of Health and Human Services, is to make cigarettes "less affordable, less accessible, and less attractive." Here are the major approaches to reducing tobacco use:

- *Advertising.* Cigarette companies were barred from advertising on television and radio in 1969. Antismoking public relations campaigns also have a long history. In 2014, for example, the Food and Drug Administration (FDA) produced a series of ads called "The Real Cost," to highlight various downsides to smoking.

- *Labeling.* The first health warning was added to cigarettes in 1965; warnings have been updated ever since. Still, the United States has milder labels and weaker warnings than many other countries.

- *Taxation.* Cigarettes are taxed at a higher rate than many other products. There are two main arguments for placing taxes on cigarettes. First, smokers place a higher strain on the health-care system than nonsmokers—that is, they cost society more than nonsmokers do. And second, taxes make cigarettes more expensive, which influences more people to quit.

A smoking lounge at an airport. Laws against smoking often have two justifications: one is to protect others from second-hand smoke, and the other is the hope that the inconvenience will convince smokers to quit.

- *Regulation of smokers.* Laws banning smoking in public places have expanded. Again, there are two main arguments for these "indoor air" laws. First, secondhand smoke damages nonsmokers, who do not ask to be exposed and may not be able to leave a particular location. Second, the inconvenience of finding a legal place to smoke is yet another way to convince people to quit.
- *Regulation of tobacco companies.* For decades, tobacco companies occupied a unique place in the United States. Although they made and sold products containing drugs that directly affected human health, they were never forced to disclose the ingredients in their products the way other drug companies were. A major step forward in this area was taken in 2009, with the passage of the Family Smoking Prevention and Tobacco Control Act. The law gives the FDA the right to regulate the ingredients in cigarettes. The medical field is especially hopeful that the FDA will force a reduction in the nicotine levels in cigarettes. Lower amounts of nicotine in cigarettes have been shown to reduce exposure levels, dependence, and the overall number of cigarettes smoked.

TEXT-DEPENDENT QUESTIONS

1. When did humans first start growing tobacco?
2. How did the tobacco industry react to reports that their product was dangerous?
3. What are some of the ways governments try to keep people from smoking or get them to quit?

RESEARCH PROJECT

Find out more about the history of cigarette regulation in the United States. Create a timeline that shows the evolution of different warning labels, for example, and the creation of various laws to limit smoking.

CHAPTER FIVE

NICOTINE—EFFECTS AND QUITTING

Nicotine is available in a variety of forms, including tobacco pipes and cigarettes for smoking, and "chaw," "dip," for chewing. People who are trying to quit might use nicotine skin patches and gum. Recently, "smokeless" cigarettes, such as the e-cigarette for "vaping," and other tobacco-free products containing nicotine have become popular.

All these formats are vehicles for transferring nicotine into the bloodstream. But they provide different amounts of nicotine. For instance, an average cigarette provides roughly one milligram of nicotine in a fairly short period of time. Chewing tobacco, on the other hand, delivers between three and five milligrams, but over a longer period of time. What many people don't realize is that nicotine is one of the most addictive

Harvesting tobacco plants in Cuba.

and deadly drugs there is—especially when it is combined with the other chemicals present in cigarettes.

HOW DOES NICOTINE WORK?

Nicotine is a chemical stimulant. It causes the brain to release a number of different neurotransmitters that have mood-altering effects. For example, dopamine is a neurotransmitter that's associated with feelings of pleasure and happiness. The neurotransmitter called norepinephrine is associated with mental alertness. This mix of different effects is very powerful, and nicotine has a direct impact on users' moods. People who depend on nicotine say that it makes them feel both mentally sharper and alert, while also making them more relaxed.

But these effects also mean that it is extremely easy to become dependent on nicotine. Despite generations of claims from the tobacco industry, the fact is that nicotine is an extremely addictive substance.

Nicotine gets into the human body very quickly, and it creates good feelings almost instantly. However, nicotine does not stay in the human body for very long. That means the person using it will want more in a pretty short time. It's also easy to build up a tolerance to nicotine, which means that your body needs more and more nicotine to get the same effects.

Meanwhile, the negative aspects of tobacco and nicotine—and there are a lot of negatives, which we'll get to below—don't appear until later. So there is a disconnect between the effects, which are immediate but brief, and the consequences, which are slower to arrive but can be devastating. Researchers have found that this is a perfect recipe to create millions of addicts.

DR. NICOTINE?

Tobacco was lauded as a wonder drug throughout history (see chapter one for more on this history). Many of the claims made on behalf of tobacco—that it could protect people from bubonic plague, for instance—were absurd. However, the nicotine in tobacco does have a powerful impact on neurotransmitters in the brain. Researchers are exploring whether it could be helpful in treating certain mental disorders, including Alzheimer's disease, attention-deficit hyperactivity disorder (ADHD), and schizophrenia.

It's important to keep in mind that research into the use of nicotine in treating mental disorders involves injections or patches that are given in a lab setting, *not casual nicotine use*. Also, the research is all preliminary. There is currently no approved medical use for nicotine. And even if nicotine is found to have medical uses, it is well established that tobacco and cigarettes, which contain a number of other hazardous chemicals, have many detrimental effects that far outweigh any potential health benefits.

THE EFFECTS OF CIGARETTES

We have come a long way from the 1950s, when industry leaders and even doctors used to claim that cigarettes were not harmful. We now know that the many risks of smoking include:

- many types of cancers, especially lung and oral cancers
- heart disease and stroke
- damage to bones
- decreased immune system function
- arthritis
- diabetes
- eye problems
- fertility problems
- premature childbirth, low-weight babies
- decrease of blood supply to the skin, causing the skin to become thinner and easily damaged

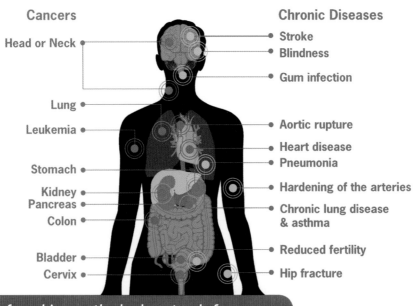

The effect of smoking on the body extends far beyond the lungs.

TOXIC INGREDIENTS

The website of the American Lung Association lists some of the toxic chemicals in cigarettes, along with their other uses. This is just a sampling:

- acetone—found in nail polish remover
- acetic acid—an ingredient in hair dye
- arsenic—used in rat poison
- butane—used in lighter fluid
- cadmium—active component in battery acid
- carbon monoxide—released in car exhaust fumes
- lead—used in batteries
- methanol—a main component in rocket fuel
- tar—material for paving roads

Source: American Lung Association, "What's in a Cigarette?" http://www.lung.org/stop-smoking/smoking-facts/whats-in-a-cigarette.html.

According to the CDC, more than 10 times as many Americans have died prematurely due to smoking than have died in all the wars the country has fought in. Almost one in five deaths in the United States is connected to smoking.

Cigarettes do not just affect the person using them, however. The smoke that results is toxic and can impact the health of nonsmokers who happen to be nearby. This phenomenon is called "secondhand smoke." The CDC reports that more than 7,000 lung cancer deaths are traceable to secondhand smoke every year. People who are regularly exposed to secondhand smoke have an increased likelihood of developing cardiovascular problems. And secondhand smoke is especially damaging to children: studies have shown that children exposed to secondhand smoke develop serious illnesses like asthma, bronchitis, and pneumonia more often than other kids.

How is it possible that one substance can have such a negative impact? One reason is that it's not just one substance. For decades, the tobacco industry fought hard to keep people from finding out what's actually in their products. But we now know that there are about 600 different ingredients in cigarettes. According to the American Lung Association, cigarette smoke contains over 7,000 chemicals, hundreds of which are considered toxic, and about 70 of which are known carcinogens (See sidebar on page 51 for a partial list.)

WHAT ABOUT E-CIGARETTES?

The latest innovation in smoking is e-cigarettes for "vaping." They come in many different designs—they can look like traditional cigarettes or pipes, for example, while some come in wild new shapes like pens or memory sticks for computers. They can also be flavored to taste like fruit, candy, or anything else the manufacturers can dream up.

Despite the variations, all e-cigarettes are fundamentally the same. They all have some sort of cartridge that holds the dose of nicotine and the flavoring, some sort of power source (usually a battery), and a method of turning the nicotine and flavoring into breathable vapor. What they do not have is actual tobacco.

The big question is, are these safer than traditional cigarettes and pipes? And the answer is, sort of. The good news is that because e-cigarettes have no tobacco, the most toxic ingredients in cigarettes are no longer present. So in that sense, yes, e-cigarettes are safer. Certainly it's safer to *not* inhale butane, lead, and carbon monoxide than it is to inhale those things. In fact, many researchers see a lot of potential for e-cigarettes in the context of what's called "harm reduction." In other words, while *not* smoking is better, research suggests that e-cigarettes are less harmful to your health than traditional cigarettes. There is also much less risk of secondhand smoke with e-cigarettes. In other words, they are a step in the right direction.

Some people worry that e-cigarettes will cause former smokers to relapse, but recent evidence does not support this concern. A 2014 study published in the journal *Nicotine & Tobacco Research* found that e-cigarette use is highest among two groups: current smokers, and those who quit within the past year. The study's authors theorized that high rates of e-cigarette use among those who quit in the past year might be due to people using e-cigarettes to help them quit. The study also found that e-cigarette use is low among former smokers who quit more than a year ago. This suggests that e-cigarettes are not causing former smokers to relapse in large numbers.

But there is a lot we don't know about the ingredients in e-cigarettes and whether they are safe. The American Lung Association reports that tests of e-cigarettes have revealed detectable levels of toxic chemicals. This is especially worrying, since e-cigarettes are so often perceived as reducing health risks. There are also a lot of questions about whether the flavorings are safe to inhale. In other words, saying that e-cigarettes may be "safer" than traditional cigarettes is not at all the same thing as saying they are "safe."

Another major concern has to do with young people. E-cigarettes flavors like chocolate, cotton candy, and bubble gum sound suspiciously like products marketed to kids. Many young people mistakenly believe that e-cigarettes are completely safe. A 2014 study in *JAMA Pediatrics* found that

An e-cigarette.

e-cigarette use was actually associated with higher rates of smoking in teens. That raises concerns that e-cigarettes might serve as a gateway to smoking in this younger age group. When they are marketed to a younger audience, e-cigarettes have the potential to get a new generation addicted to nicotine.

GETTING FREE

Most people know by now that using nicotine is unhealthy. If it's that bad, why do people continue to smoke? Many people try to quit and fail many times before finally succeeding. According to the American Cancer Society, the average smoker will attempt to quit three times before quitting for good. It has been observed that tobacco is as difficult to quit as any "hard" drug, such as heroin.

Quitting smoking (or other tobacco products) can cause an extreme craving for nicotine that can feel very unpleasant. Smokers' bodies come to expect regular doses of nicotine, and when the drug does not arrive, their bodies experience withdrawal symptoms like dizziness, exhaustion, headaches, and very bad moods.

There are a number of options to help ease the craving for nicotine. The approach with the most support is called nicotine replacement therapy (NRT). The idea of NRT is to help wean the smoker's body off nicotine gradually. There are gums and lozenges that people can chew that deliver small amounts of nicotine into the bloodstream. There are also patches, which look like stickers but are actually medical adhesives that deliver nicotine through the skin.

In addition to NRT, there are other prescription medications that can help ease withdrawal symptoms, like Zyban (which is actually an antidepressant called bupropion) and Chantix (varenicline). Yoga and exercise have been shown to help ease nicotine cravings, so these may

A QUIT PLAN

Experts say that smokers are more likely to stay with their decision to quit if they plan ahead. The following is a summary of a "quit plan" from the National Cancer Institute":

- Pick a quit date. Rather than quitting on a whim, pick a date and spend time thinking about how you will quit.

- Let people know you are quitting. As the date approaches, tell friends, family, and coworkers that you are quitting so they can support you.

- Get rid of things that remind you of smoking. Make sure to throw out all ashtrays, lighters, and anything else that was a part of your habit. If possible, try to get rid of the smoke smell in your clothes, car, and home—just the smell of cigarettes can bring on cravings in regular users.

- Make a list of the reasons you're quitting, and keep the list where you can see it.

- Identify your triggers. Think about the people, places, and situations that make you want to smoke. As the quit date approaches, make a plan to avoid these triggers.

- Plan for withdrawal. The first few days of quitting are the most difficult physically, so plan accordingly. Long-term smokers should talk to their doctors about dealing with the initial withdrawal phase.

- Reward yourself. As the National Cancer Society says, "Quitting smoking happens one minute, one hour, one day at a time." Some people like to set aside the money they *would* have spent on cigarettes and buy themselves something else. In any case, reward yourself for meeting milestones like the first 24 hours, first week, and first month without smoking.

Making a plan ahead of time can help people be successful when they attempt to quit smoking.

be a good addition to whatever method a smoker is using. Some people champion alternative remedies to reduce cravings, including hypnosis, acupuncture, and therapies with magnets, herbs, and even lasers. However, there is currently no scientific proof about the effectiveness of these strategies.

Those treatments all address the physical addiction. But, as we've said, there's more to smoking than just the physical addiction. Smokers often find that their habit has become an integral part of their daily routines. It's a part of taking breaks from work or studying, hanging out with friends, or finishing a meal. Many people say that the psychological dependence on smoking is just as hard, or even harder, to kick than the physical dependence.

Behavioral treatments, either alone or in combination with NRT, are recommended to help people deal with the psychological side of quitting. These treatments help people recognize "triggers," which are situations where they are at higher risk of wanting to smoke. Behavioral treatments also encourage coping strategies that help people learn to manage stress without smoking. It is also helpful to find social support for staying off cigarettes.

TEXT-DEPENDENT QUESTIONS

1. What are the two main components of nicotine addiction?
2. What are some positive and negative aspects of e-cigarettes?
3. What is a quit plan, and what steps does it involve?

RESEARCH PROJECT

Find out more about the effects of smoking. You might start with the website of the American Lung Association (http://www.lung.org/), as well as other sources listed in the back of this book. Make a poster or pamphlet that explains the risks.

FURTHER READING

BOOKS AND ARTICLES

Brandt, Allan M. *The Cigarette Century: The Rise, Fall, and Deadly Persistence of the Product That Defined America.* New York: Basic Books, 2007.

Friedman, Lauri S., ed. *Alcohol.* Introducing Issues with Opposing Viewpoints series. Farmington Hills, MI: Greenhaven, 2010.

Gately, Iain. *Drink: A Cultural History of Alcohol.* New York: Gotham, 2008.

Kuhn, Cynthia, Scott Swartzwelder, and Wilkie Wilson. *Buzzed: The Straight Facts about the Most Used and Abused Drugs from Alcohol to Ecstasy.* 4th ed. New York: W. W. Norton, 2014.

Oreskes, Naomi and Erik M. Conway. *Merchants of Doubt: How a Handful of Scientists Obscured the Truth on Issues from Tobacco Smoke to Global Warming.* New York: Bloomsbury, 2010.

ONLINE

Alcoholics Anonymous. "What is A.A.?" http://www.aa.org/pages/en_US/what-is-aa.

National Institute on Alcohol Abuse and Alcoholism. "Underage Drinking." http://www.niaaa.nih.gov/alcohol-health/special-populations-co-occurring-disorders/underage-drinking.

TeensHealth. "Alcohol." http://kidshealth.org/teen/drug_alcohol/alcohol/alcohol.html.

TeensHealth. "Smoking." http://kidshealth.org/teen/cancer_center/q_a/smoking.html.

World Health Organization. *Tobacco Explained: The Truth about the Tobacco Industry . . . in Its Own Words.* http://www.who.int/tobacco/media/en/TobaccoExplained.pdf.

EDUCATIONAL VIDEOS

Access these videos with your smartphone or use the URLs below to find them online.

 "Under Construction: Alcohol and the Teenage Brain," TurningPointTraining. "Discusses adolescent brain development and highlights the effects of alcohol and risky drinking on different brain regions, as well as its impact on behaviour." https://youtu.be/g2gVzVIBc_g

 "How Alcohol Affects Your Brain And Body," Business Insider. "Alcohol is one of the most dangerous substances on the planet. Someone dies from alcohol use every ten seconds, and one night of binge drinking can take a huge toll on your immune system." https://youtu.be/VAlE-UESTOA

 "No Joke: The Truth About Alcoholism," The Late Late Show with Craig Ferguson. "Featuring Robin Williams, Anthony Hopkins, Bill Cosby and Craig Ferguson." https://youtu.be/rs5QHWMLATI

 "Nicotine and tobacco addiction," National Institute on Drug Abuse. "NIDA scientists Gaya Dowling and Redonna Chandler talk about the health effects and dangers on smoking and nicotine." https://youtu.be/DqLA2sW_thw

 "Teens Using E-cigarettes More Likely to Start Smoking Tobacco," National Institute on Drug Abuse. "NIDA Director Dr. Nora Volkow discusses NIH-funded study which shows possible link between teen's use of e-cigarettes and initiation of tobacco use." https://youtu.be/t6VgxxIbTwg

SERIES GLOSSARY

abstention: actively choosing to not do something.

acute: something that is intense but lasts a short time.

alienation: a sense of isolation or detachment from a larger group.

alleviate: to lessen or relieve.

binge: doing something to excess.

carcinogenic: something that causes cancer.

chronic: ongoing or recurring.

cognitive: having to do with thought.

compulsion: a desire that is very hard or even impossible to resist.

controlled substance: a drug that is regulated by the government.

coping mechanism: a behavior a person learns or develops in order to manage stress.

craving: a very strong desire for something.

decriminalized: something that is not technically legal but is no longer subject to prosecution.

depressant: a substance that slows particular bodily functions.

detoxify: to remove toxic substances (such as drugs or alcohol) from the body.

ecosystem: a community of living things interacting with their environment.

environment: one's physical, cultural, and social surroundings.

genes: units of inheritance that are passed from parent to child and contain information about specific traits and characteristics.

hallucinate: seeing things that aren't there.

hyperconscious: to be intensely aware of something.

illicit: illegal; forbidden by law or cultural custom.

inhibit: to limit or hold back.

interfamilial: between and among members of a family.

metabolize: the ability of a living organism to chemically change compounds.

neurotransmitter: a chemical substance in the brain.

paraphernalia: the equipment used for producing or ingesting drugs, such as pipes or syringes.

physiological: relating to the way an organism functions.

placebo: a medication that has no physical effect and is used to test whether new drugs actually work.

predisposition: to be more inclined or likely to do something.

prohibition: when something is forbidden by law.

recidivism: a falling back into past behaviors, especially criminal ones.

recreation: something done for fun or enjoyment.

risk factors: behaviors, traits, or influences that make a person vulnerable to something.

sobriety: the state of refraining from alcohol or drugs.

social learning: a way that people learn behaviors by watching other people.

stimulant: a class of drug that speeds up bodily functions.

stressor: any event, thought, experience, or biological or chemical function that causes a person to feel stress.

synthetic: made by people, often to replicate something that occurs in nature.

tolerance: the state of needing more of a particular substance to achieve the same effect.

traffic: to illegally transport people, drugs, or weapons to sell throughout the world.

withdrawal: the physical and psychological effects that occur when a person with a use disorder suddenly stops using substances.

INDEX

ABOUT THE AUTHOR

H.W. Poole is a writer and editor of books for young people, such as the multivolume sets *Mental Illnesses and Disorders* and *Families in the 21st Century* (Mason Crest). She is also responsible for many critically acclaimed reference books, including *Political Handbook of the World* (CQ Press) and the *Encyclopedia of Terrorism* (SAGE). She was coauthor and editor of the *History of the Internet* (ABC-CLIO), which won the 2000 American Library Association RUSA award.

ABOUT THE ADVISOR

Sara Becker, Ph.D. is a clinical researcher and licensed clinical psychologist specializing in the treatment of adolescents with substance use disorders. She is an Assistant Professor (Research) in the Center for Alcohol and Addictions Studies at the Brown School of Public Health and the Evaluation Director of the New England Addiction Technology Transfer Center. Dr. Becker received her Ph.D. in Clinical Psychology from Duke University and completed her clinical residency at Harvard Medical School's McLean Hospital. She joined the Center for Alcohol and Addictions Studies as a postdoctoral fellow and transitioned to the faculty in 2011. Dr. Becker directs a program of research funded by the National Institute on Drug Abuse that explores novel ways to improve the treatment of adolescents with substance use disorders. She has authored over 30 peer-reviewed publications and book chapters and serves on the Editorial Board of the *Journal of Substance Abuse Treatment*.

PHOTO CREDITS